Lost in Reverie

Lost in Reverie

A Vision Through the Prism of Life

SUDEEP KR. BANERJEE

PARTRIDGE

To order additional copies of this book, contact
Partridge India
000 800 10062 62
orders.india@partridgepublishing.com

www.partridgepublishing.com/india

Contents

Acknowledgement

This collection of poetry is dedicated to my dear grandfather - **Late. Rabindra Nath Banerjee** who encouraged me to compose poems at a very early age. He was extremely creative in his poetic works and had an exceptional vocabulary.

Miss you *"Dadun"!!*

I am indebted to my wife - **Jayashree Banerjee** - my pillar of support, who has always stood by my side at times of happiness and distress. It is because of her constant encouragement that I restarted writing after a gap of 15 years.

I also thank one and all who have influenced, rather transformed me into the person I am today and for changing my perspective towards life altogether.

1

Return To the Roots

With the last file signed & dispatched,
    Bid goodbye to my loyal black chair.
Old must give way to the new,
    Is a rule of nature truly & squarely fair.

Next day was a new beginning,
    As I moved to my very native place.
The village I grew up in,
    Before joining the mad corporate race.

I was glad to be back,
    Amidst folks and friends.
Though lot did change here,
    Including lifestyle and trends.

Once a sleepy village,
    Now a smart happening town.
But with its old charm missing,
    My enthusiasm went down.

My favourite childhood friends,
    Lacked the warmth & zeal.
And interaction with my relatives,
    Left me with a sad unwelcome feel.

So I packed up my bags once again,
　　　This time to travel till I could tour no more.
Visiting unfamiliar places, making new friends,
　　　Riding mighty waves; treading pristine sandy
shores.

My roots certainly don't belong,
　　　To one village out of memory.
But it does feels great to be a "World Citizen",
　　　And it is better to be late than sorry!

2
Haunting

Since the day we finally moved,
    To this old, secluded log house.
It has been an endless pursuit,
    A typical race of cat and mouse.

I often felt while sleeping,
    Someone yanking away my quilt.
Any protest was responded with,
    Gentle creepy tickle on my feet.

I needed a strong evidence,
    Wanting desperately to move out.
Tried explaining to one & all,
    But my Dad surely had his own set of doubts.

It actually started happening,
    On a late Saturday night,
When all the guests had left,
    And my Mom shirked in fright.

Pointing at the shadowy creatures,
    She yelled at the top of her lungs.
Things started falling off from kitchen shelves -
    Cups, dishes, bottles & ice tongs!

Then it stopped,
     All at once.
We froze in horror,
     In a state of trance.

We couldn't sleep,
     At all that night.
But then my Dad realized,
     My genuine plight.

A priest arrived,
     The very next day.
He blessed our house,
     And asked us to pray.

Though nothing changed,
     We adapted to stay.
With falling objects,
     And those weird creatures at play!

3

The Casuarina Tree

Stood silently in its forlorn melancholy,
    Overlooking the castle with no one left to care.
However it was truly a dear companion,
    Of the little princess who once lived there.

But it was over a hundred years ago,
    When her little hands had sown the seed.
Had watered it regularly,
    Taking care of its every need.

Quickly as it grew,
    From a weak sapling to a tree.
It saw the little princess,
    Turn into a dame of unfathomable beauty.

And it still remembers,
    The starry night.
When the moon shone high,
    Round, full and bright.

The princes had waited unwearyingly,
    All through the night.
Till her beloved came secretly,
    And the two embraced in delight.

It also remembers,
    The very fateful day,
When the nemeses attacked,
    And her soldiers fled away.

The king was assassinated,
    In cold blood.
And Oh dear lord,
    Not a soul was spared.

When the princes was dragged,
    Out of the grand castle,
She kept her head high,
    And her eyes still dazzled.

Alas! When she was slain,
    And her poor soul was set free.
Still clasped in her blood stained hands,
    Was a branch of her favourite casuarina tree!

4

Enchanted

I rose up from my own body,
    As light as air could be.
I walked away from my own self,
    Which was at rest as I could see.

My steps led me to the windows,
    From where I watched the sky.
Snowy with stars it was,
    A beauty no rich could buy.

Then the clock struck two,
    And I knew it was time.
For the angel of love to come,
    In whose arms I could entwine.

She tip-toed into my room,
    And gently came to me.
As usual she looked tenderly beautiful,
    As I had expected to see.

To see her eyes that spoke to me,
    The softest of emotions ever.
To feel the flocks of hair unlocked,
    Cascading down her shoulders.

To seal her lips that quivered,
        To utter what her eyes meant to say.
With a kiss everlasting and eternal,
        And even lifetime is too short to state.

Then she honoured my affectionate arms,
        With an incredibly delicate embrace.
That instantly tranquillized my restless soul,
        With its typical quality of solace.

So I returned to my native body,
        With a feeling of satisfaction within.
The mere thought of being with her,
        Was truly very soothing.

As a rule she comes to me,
        Every night in my dreams.
And I can feel her aroma even when,
        She's left me alone to scream!

5

Death

There are things that makes us think,
    During every moment of our life.
But we're so much lost in our daily chores,
    We hardly think of the end of life.

Many are scared of death,
    Some think they'll live forever.
As if death is for others,
    It won't happen to them, never ever.

For someone who's been a failure,
    Every time, everywhere,
Death is a bliss he wishes to embrace,
    Silently without fear.

While there are others who believe,
    Death & taxes are both inevitable.
Therefore they accept it somehow,
    Surely their nerves are stable.

There are few who make fun of death,
     Never fear to die.
Having lived to their heart's content,
     Happily do they lie.

For me death is a state of mind,
     As true & necessary life could be.
I happily wish to cajole death,
     That would really set me free!

6
The Black Beetle

It buzzed, it moved & caught my eyes,
    It paused, then crawled & tried to fly.
It made its way through the air,
    Slowly, unsteadily as its wings could steer.

But soon its weight brought it down,
    Like a leaking gas balloon.
Buzzing & dancing all along,
    In tune with its inspiring song

Then it flew once again,
    Hit the roof, the wall and the window panes.
It crashed to the floor upside down,
    And all its antics made me frown.

But, I was amused to see it try,
    Correcting its posture without a cry.
I forgot my setbacks, the distress and pain,
    My smile had returned once again.

Then before by eyes; I saw it happen,
    He stepped on it and I was shaken.
To see its little quivering body smeared to the ground,
    And the cruel feet that killed it without a sound.

7

Fait Accompli

The rays of light pierced through the windows,
    And lit the innocent face.
The radiance, the gleam was all still there,
    That added to his triumphant grace.

The forehead bore no frown,
    And proud were the grey hair.
That had witnessed changing seasons,
    And vicissitudes of eventful eighty years.

No more days of struggle,
    And no solitary days of stress.
The glorious days of romance,
    And the matchless heroic ways!

No more sins to regret,
    No more wrongs to fear.
His selfless deeds were endless,
    And his soul was crystal clear.

So as he lay,
    Like a warrior dead.
Stood by his side,
    Were his foes and friends.

Needless to say,
    He had won their hearts.
Who now cried,
    In fits and starts.

As they followed the hearse,
    Memories haunted them for real –
Of togetherness, fun, frolic, cajoling or even reproach,
    Something or the other everyone did feel.

At last the pyre was set ablaze,
    Whose leaping flames shrouded the martyr.
A man who lived and died like a warrior,
    Had nothing more to care.

8
Life in a City

Years ago when he first landed,
    Into the grand, beautiful city.
Penniless, yet brimming with confidence,
    He never accepted anyone's pity!

With no real friends,
    No serious inspiration available.
He decided to undertake with perfection,
    Just any job that came to his table.

He toiled tirelessly night & day,
    Amassing goodwill, blessings, trust & wealth.
His rise from rags to riches was not easy,
    But only few valued his style of working in stealth.

There was no time for family,
    Hardly any moments of carefree fun.
Recollections of childhood were plenty,
    But the quagmire had made it impossible to run.

The risks were too many & high,
    Mostly materialistic or financial.
The routine, the chase, the competition,
    But were they indeed so crucial?

It was time for self-introspection,
    About his real expectations in life.
Different emotions started building up,
    And began hurting him like a knife.

Realizing he was actually needed elsewhere,
    He firmly decided to retrace his trail.
And he was sure, he won't be missing at all,
    The monotony, his peers, the city & the metro rail.

9
The Solitary Wave

It roared then muffled,
    As it rushed to the shore.
Clattered and clamoured,
    Into the rocks and stones.

Trusting in its destiny,
    To be honest and fair.
Hastened its journey,
    With a force beyond compare.

It danced its way all along,
    In tune with its cadenced song.
The albatross, the fish and even the dolphins cheered,
    All through a journey undoubtedly weird.

They relied on it,
    At their times of need.
As it sheltered them without prejudice,
    Countless kinds of every breed.

The moment it knew,
     The shore was near.
All had left,
     Its near & dear.

Thus it lost its glory,
     As it dashed to the shore.
Lifeless, lonely and forgotten
     Like never before.

       …….   Only to be born again!

10

Jogger's Park

The morning gale,
>   Was a welcome treat.
On a summer day,
>   Without its usual heat.

It was early,
>   Yet it was time.
For morning joggers,
>   Who waited in line.

Till the instructor arrived,
>   In her smart pink shorts.
While the oldies squirmed,
>   In total discomfort.

Then the Joggers jogged,
>   The walkers walked.
The elderly lectured,
>   On what was not.

Children raced on their sporty bikes,
>   Along the slippery cycling track.
Unexpectedly the leader lost his balance,
>   And hit the ground on his back.

The ladies too,
>Had their piece of fun.
As they gossiped about the teens,
>Who had eloped in a garbage van.

Soon it was noon,
>And the noisy hawkers arrived.
Selling hotdogs, candyfloss,
>Sweet corns & dumplings fried.

Before long; it was dusk,
>And the sun went down.
It thus became peaceful again,
>In my sleepy little town.

11

Another Chance

Once a sportsman,
>And a champion too.
But today I'm helpless,
>What else can I do?

A sedentary life,
>Is something I'm forced to live.
The society owes me nothing,
>Nor do I have anything to give.

I feast when I am happy,
>I gorge when I am sad.
I'm obese, sick, possibly dying,
>Or perhaps it's not all that bad.

Resting lazily on my couch,
>As I watch my favourite channel on sports.
Cherish the days I used to play,
>The trophies I won at the tennis court.

The crash left me crippled,
      Lonely, battered and hollow.
Wish I had a true motivation to live,
      And a real inspiration to follow.

Given a real chance to prove again,
      I swear to make a swift comeback.
There's only one thing I must toil on,
      It's just the confidence that I lack!

      .... Once a winner, always a winner. **Just Try**!

12
Being in Love

A phase of life has just begun,
    Like a pleasant breeze before a storm.
Everything wrong seems to be right,
    Everything right appears to be wrong.

Soon you will find,
    Your heart to be kind.
And feel her presence,
    A bliss divine.

Then the shroud of passion,
    Will consume your heart to dash on.
As you start to love each other,
    The whole world will come to bother.

Must bear the curses and plentiful disapproving verses,
    In the whispers of people around.
You still must smile at them without prejudice,
    To prove your love as mature, true & profound.

Wait not for the returns,
>	Wait not for your day.
For your day will come when it must,
>	To sweep all your sorrows away.

You may then have her,
>	All through your life by your side.
As the nightmare will perish,
>	You will be awake with your eyes open wide.

13

Fantasia

Clatters the cloud in its glory,
>   Breaks the silence of the night.
Shakes the world in its fury,
>   And then pours down with delight.

The roars of thunder,
>   The black dark sky,
The deafening silence,
>   And the solitude nearby.

The cracking of firewood,
>   The rising flame.
Ignites my desire,
>   Her single name.

I wish to have her,
>   In my arms.
In all her beauty,
>   And her charms.

And the time stands still,
    For a little while.
To witness our love,
    And her delicate smile.

Then I awake,
    From my trance.
That's the end,
    Of thunder, lightning & romance

14

Yester Years

It was a breezy Sunday evening,
      When the unique cycle bell rang,
It was an ingenious code we invented,
      To call members of the "Legendary" bikers gang.

It meant that it was time,
      To hop on the bicycle and hit the playground.
That was full of children like us,
      Busy riding the swing, the sledge & the
merry-go-round.

Old, friendly Bruno would bark incessantly,
      As its owner reined it for a walk.
And we wished it played with us,
      Till we finally left the park.

The game of cricket,
      Never ended without a fight.
Between those who got a chance to bat,
      And those who lost their right.

Silly games appeared seriously unfair at times,
      Advice from elders sounded like an offensive curse.
Little did we comprehend then,
      That real life was even damn worse!

It seems like yesterday,
        When I was down with fever.
My friends flocked around tirelessly,
        And the games waited till I recovered.

Can't think of such camaraderie,
        Can't imagine a love so pure.
In a world of matured grownups,
        Indifferent, selfish, hard to endure

Wish I had the magic wand,
        That could transform me to a cheerful kid once
again.
I'd dare not barter my childhood ever,
        In exchange for a life of meaningless stress,
jealousy & insufferable pain

15

Eternal Friendship

Days will come and days will go,
    The list of memories shall always grow.
Deep in our hearts, safe in our minds,
    They will remain ever so.

The days of laughter,
    The days of pain.
The days of sunshine,
    The days of rain.

Even though you will be away from me,
    Our memories will always be there.
To stir the emotions lying within,
    Moistening my eyes with tears.

But I know it's time,
    For us to part.
For a new phase of life,
    Has to start.

You were always by my side,
    When I needed you the most.
But soon you will gone far away,
    Leaving me with an exemplary friendship to boast!

16

Lost in the Woods

As I briskly walked along,
  Humming, whistling my native song.
I raced my steps on the mountain track,
  Tirelessly carrying a heavy nap-sack.

It was picturesque,
  As I looked around.
The trees, the thickets, the birds & bees,
  The rocky cliff & the wild sea.

As I strode quickly & trekked anon,
  Saw a deer cuddling its fawn.
But soon I knew that I was lost,
  Then the jungle was shrouded in the winter frost.

The sun set down,
  And it was night.
A python hissed,
  And I shrieked in fright.

Then the sound of footsteps,
  Took me unawares.
I stared at her,
  But devoid of fears.

As I rubbed my eyes,
  In utter disbelief.
I knew I had awakened,
  From an indelible sleep.

17

The Lightning

The sun had set,
    And the moon did shine.
Which the cloud soon covered,
    With its silver line.

Then there was silence,
    For a little while.
The village looked deserted,
    From a distant mile.

Little girl Tina,
    Was happily playing indoors.
Obeying her mother,
    By not venturing to the moors.

The silence was broken,
    And it started to rain.
The thunder was loud,
    Like a lion in pain.

The wrath of nature,
     Was certainly inevitable.
The lightning did strike,
     And the hut was in shambles.

When everything stopped,
     Nothing was found.
But for poor little Tina,
     Buried to the ground.

18

Just Asking!

When the sun is out,
>And the day has just begun.
Why then appears the cloud,
>To cover the innocent sun?

When there's cry for rain,
>The drought has just begun.
Why the troubles are endless,
>Aren't there answers to none?

Money buys time,
>And promises great returns.
Then why does our heart still ache,
>If it was really so much fun?

There's pleasure in some eyes,
>To see the weak weep.
Is the animal within us so powerful?
>That humanity dare not speak?

Nothing stops us from hurting others,
>Wealth outweighs love away.
A blue Cadillac but a broken heart,
>Is that the price to be paid anyway?

Why then run after a known mirage,
       Breaking hearts all along?
A track stained with blood & tears,
       Of innocent, harmless, near and dear

What it costs to be humble,
       What it costs to be kind?
Why there's hatred everywhere,
       True love is something one hardly finds... Tell
me why?

19

Souvenir of Life

It was born and brought to earth,
    With a heart which had a small hole.
Despite the condition her mother had vowed,
    To take care of her poor thing, a nameless soul.

Its heart did beat for a little while,
    Then it stopped & was calm.
Whilst her mother held her angel,
    Tightly in her affectionate arms.

Then she wailed,
    And cried in pain,
Cursed the heavens,
    In utmost remorse & disdain.

She hugged and kissed the lifeless form,
    Suddenly she could hear it breathe.
She wiped her tears, couldn't believe her ears,
    Because it was a true miracle indeed!

20

Yet Another Day

The winter snow,
    The summer breeze,
Blossoming spring,
    The rainy days.

All these seasons,
    Have their reasons.
But one must quit,
    Ones self-made prisons.

And you would know,
    What life really has to offer!
The priceless joys in nature's ploys,
    Hidden overtly in its coffer.

Material wealth,
    Social Pride.
Professional success,
    An endless stride.

And before you know,
    You've missed it all.
It's time to wake up,
    And take a call.

Share the laughter,
    Share the pain.
Celebrate your life now,
    For you never know you'll be born again!

21

A Blissful State of Love

There's a flame that burns high,
    In my heart that holds.
The desire that diminishes not,
    But increases manifolds.

Mere thought of her; paralyses my body,
    The very sight of her; makes me fly.
Her amazing voice; nails me down,
    Wish we could talk forever; till I die.

In my dreams she comes,
    And plays with my soul.
She teases me every now and then,
    But the night ends too soon.

And when I awake,
    She's not there!
Wish my dreams were endless,
    With no dawns to fear!

So, this flame of love in me,
     Calls out to The!
Make thy world a paradise,
     Where all can remain free.

Where Your blessings are truly countless,
     Where people live to love.
Where their earnest desires get fulfilled,
     And their prayers reach thy God above!

22

The Hang Man

The kerchief dropped,
    The leaver screeched.
The noose tightened,
    And a soul was released.

Psycho or innocent,
    Guilty or framed.
Unprejudiced I execute,
    My emotions restrained.

I do not judge,
    I do not cry.
But tears do swell up and trickle,
    Down wrinkled corners of my tired eyes.

As I walk along the city streets,
    Attending to my daily chores.
Notice the frowns and the hateful looks,
    Unwelcome vibes at the shopping stores.

I do not judge,
    I do not cry.
Only wish these people,
    Could give it a try!

And they'd realize for sure,
　　　What it actually takes.
To cause death to an unknown,
　　　For mere duty's sake.

It's the smile on the faces of my little folks,
　　　The daily bread undoubtedly brings.
Makes my life-clock tick without a break,
　　　Overlooking the unpleasant things!

23

Parking Lot

Weekdays are chaotic,
    Particularly Mondays are bad.
When bumpers hit one another,
    Their drivers turn mad.

On a typical weekend afternoon,
    When the crowd is marginally low.
Parking becomes easier & comfortable,
    For new drivers who are relatively slow.

Shady spots & remote corners,
    Are amongst the most preferred sites,
For young pairs in cars with tinted glasses,
    And those riding noisy superbikes.

Seen many dramatic moments,
    Both happy & sad unfold here.
Duets proposing with total honesty,
    And some parting ways in despair.

Have seen few people
    Who went out of their way to help, many a times ,
And their little acts of kindness,
    Most certainly didn't cost them a dime.

Some incidents are remarkable,
     And worth mentioning here.
Repaying acts of kindness in ones blood,
     Not every man or woman would dare.

The local heartless goon called Rob,
     Surprised everybody one day.
When he helped an old lady rise,
     Who had stumbled at the parking bay.

A year later cops came scouting for Rob,
     The sound of spraying bullets echoed through
the air.
Rob surrendered unhurt, consenting to an everlasting
guilt,
     Whilst the old lady, on his behalf lay dead out
there.

Isn't it a stirring story?
     Well, its totally up to you, believe it or not.
And if you have any desire to know more,
     Meet "Rob" himself at the same Parking lot!

24

The Monsoon Fair

With dark clouds looming above,
    And occasional flashes illuminating the murky sky.
The sporadic rains had no impact,
    On folks who had been waiting for mid of July!

Every year during this time,
    There's an awesome festivity in the air.
As young and old gather without fail,
    To attend their native "Monsoon Fair".

You cannot miss the funny clowns,
    Who greet you warmly at the entry gates.
Followed by a corridor of stalls,
    Selling knick-knacks at reasonable rates.

You can see the children merrily riding,
    The giant wheel, the swings & the
merry-go-round.
And pity those on the scary roller coaster,
    Screaming loud while hanging upside down.

After a daring yet exciting ride,
    One feels hungry to the core.
And there are abundant options,
    Available at every food store.

Right from juices, to burgers,
　　Nachos, Hotdogs, dumplings or rolls.
The delightful steamed sweet corns,
　　Even healthy chicken soup in Chinese bowls.

As the rain suddenly reappears,
　　People run scouting for cover.
Activities do stop temporarily,
　　And springs back to normal once it's over.

When the sun sets down,
　　Behind the heavy dark grey clouds.
The ground lights up beautifully,
　　While the clamour gets even more loud.

The oldest couple in their eighty's,
　　Were a regular visitor to the fair.
Hand in hand they strolled the ground,
　　Ignoring people with curious stares.

Wish I could visit the fair once again,
　　As I always did, every year.
And my grand old lady wouldn't be sulking,
　　Sitting alone in my black armchair.

25
Truth

We've been taught to be Truthful,
    Right from our childhood days.
Now when I think of defining Truth,
    It just blows my mind away!

Is truth what we presume to be true?
    Or is it what people generally consider it to be?
Can every book written be considered factual?
    Or should we only rely on what we actually see?

Heard many a times from people around,
    It is always more than what meets the eye.
Isn't it also believed to be true?
    That half truth is nothing but a lie!

Are we then talking about the "Real Truth"?
    Or its interpretation which can easily vary.
The version of truth can thus change manifolds,
    And that's my real cause of worry!

Isn't Truth expected to be true?
      At all times, no matter what.
And no amount of human influence,
      Could ever change its worth.

You may call the Sun as Moon,
      Rename the mighty ocean as tree.
It doesn't change the reality a bit,
      That's what I expect "Truth" to be!

                              - Real Truth is Universal!

26

The Last Meal

The family gathered,
> When the clock struck nine.
And the food was served,
> As it was dinner time.

Children were playful,
> With the forks and spoons.
While they waited for Joe,
> To join them soon.

Granny was ready,
> With her complaints too.
Although she knew,
> There was nothing actually Joe could do.

Everybody smiled,
> As Joe took his seat.
And raised a toast,
> Before starting to eat.

He praised Mary,
> For the delicious meal,
And there were tears in his eyes,
> He could clearly feel.

He wished he could stay,
       For yet another day.
But for the call of duty,
       That came in his way.

He looked at his family,
       As he walked to the door.
He knew in his heart,
       He would see them no more.

Serving the nation,
       Has its own price.
And our Joe never dithered,
       While making the supreme sacrifice.

Every night at the dinner table,
       To this very day,
The family yearns for Joe's return,
       From the land of war, far away.

27

Till Death Do Us Part

It was a strange feeling,
    As their eyes meet by chance.
They smiled infectiously,
    At their very second glance.

They spoke without a sound,
    Oblivious to the maddening crowd.
The attraction was mutual,
    Yet both held on to their own ground.

Almost immediately the impasse was broken,
    Both shaken to their very core.
The emotional surge seemed irrepressible,
    Something they had never felt before.

Introduction was quick yet unforgettable,
    As they promptly vowed to meet again.
Their world seemed bright & beautiful,
    Amid thunder lightening & the incessant rain.

Mutual admiration turned into friendship,
    Friendship translated into unfathomable love.
Every meeting transformed their lives,
    As if sanctioned straight from the Heaven above.

Soon days became months,
　　Months turned into years.
Their relation matured with time,
　　Despite endless threats & fears.

Then one fine day,
　　Sense of realism prevailed.
In a crusade between love and practicality,
　　It's frail, naive love that miserably failed.

With emotions dried & totally wasted,
　　Not once did they listen to their hearts.
Whilst their solemn vow lost its place,
　　Which once truly meant – "Till death do us part!"

28
Soul

The tenure ended,
    At its ordained time.
The ride was rhythmic,
    Like a poetic rhyme.

Now juxtaposed total peace,
    Unfamiliar, weird yet utterly desirable.
No visible uncertainties,
    As everything looks perfectly stable.

No name, no gender,
    No religion or caste to defend,
No identity of being rich or poor,
    No consequence of being straight or bent.

No language, no hunger,
    No fatigue, no race.
No deadlines, no responsibility,
    No love, no hate.

A ceaseless state,
    Of knowing thy true self.
Through timeless introspection,
    Without any cue or genuine help.

The self evaluation is ultimate,
　　And the final judgement is what one asks.
To be born again as a valuable being.
　　To accomplish ones' unfinished tasks.

The cycle must continue,
　　Till reason to be born exists no more.
And one can finally rest till eternity,
　　Exiting through the salvation door!

29

Marooned

A perilous night just ended,
    At the very split of dawn.
Bodies & debris piled up on the shore,
    But the whole plane was gone!

With no strength left in me,
    I lay motionless on the white sands.
My body ached like hell,
    And I could barely move my hands.

To escape the blazing Sun,
    I crawled up to the nearest shade.
Blessed my stars to be alive,
    And not floating amongst those dead.

Soon contentment turned into despair,
    As I was the only man practically alive.
On an island totally obscure & desolate,
    Though full of coconut trees with beehives.

Soon hunger pangs outdid my gloom,
    But to look for food, I had to stand.
And as I tried, I trembled and fell,
    Luckily on the wet cushiony sand.

When the pain finally subsided,
        I decided to get up and attempted to walk.
I rummaged through the wreckage,
        But finding canned food & water was just sheer
luck.

I guess I survived over a month now,
        Watching ships sailing far away.
Its hope against hope but I still hope,
        Help would certainly arrive some day.

It has been an endless wait; now as I write,
        I might further endure a week or two.
And if you found this note in the floating bottle,
I am sure you would come to my rescue!
.... **Won't you?**

30
The Stranger

Where did he come from,
And where he planned to go.
No one appeared to bother,
Fully engrossed in the show.

Partly blocking the narrow exit door,
He stood reclining by the side wall.
The black woollen coat & the gloves he wore,
Not matching the warm weather at all.

Adding extra grandeur to his persona,
Was the stylish felt hat and black silk bow.
His rich cologne filled the air completely,
As he swaggered towards the front row.

I figured that he was amply opulent,
And could buy the cinema if he had to.
But he untiringly stood by the wall,
Wondered what he was seriously up to.

I thought someone would surely object,
    As he pulled out and lit his classy cigar.
But no one seemed to notice & utter a word,
    So I decided to challenge this mysterious avatar.

Just when I was about to dare him,
    For smoking in a public theatre.
The lights came up unexpectedly,
    And to my shock he wasn't even there!!